DEAD HEAT THE '69 RYDER CUP CLASSIC

PAUL TREVILLION

DEAD HEAT
THE '69 RYDER CUP
CLASSIC

 STANLEY PAUL | LONDON

STANLEY PAUL & CO LTD
178-202 Great Portland Street, London W1
AN IMPRINT OF THE HUTCHINSON GROUP

*London Melbourne Sydney Auckland
Bombay Toronto Johannesburg New York*

First published 1969

*This book has been set in Imprint, printed in Great Britain
by Taylor Garnett Evans & Co. Ltd, Watford, Herts and
bound by Wm. Brendon & Son Ltd, Tiptree, Essex*

09 102030 1

CONTENTS

Photographs by Frank Gardner

Sam Snead and Eric Brown, rival team captains, hold the Ryder Cup trophy after the greatest golf match ever staged in the forty-two years the series has been played.

FOREWORD BY ERIC BROWN, BRITISH RYDER CUP TEAM CAPTAIN

In all my years in golf, and remember I played at Lindrick in '57 when we won the Ryder Cup, I've never known such a tremendous contest as this year's match at Royal Birkdale, surely the greatest ever played. I, personally, would never want to live through those last exciting stages again. The tension on that final afternoon was hardly bearable and it is impossible to believe that this level of excitement and drama will ever quite be equalled again.

Looking back I can honestly say that I never once, at any stage during the match, thought that we would lose. We got off to a great start which I knew was all important and we kept it up throughout —but only just. Here at last was a British team which really rose to the occasion; the brilliant individual performances created an electrically charged atmosphere amongst the crowd, who sensed victory and gave tremendous support. One or two spectators were possibly a little too partisan, but then I have played Ryder Cup matches in America, and the crowds over there have not been exactly quiet. All of the boys in the team were spurred on by this vocal support, even if it may have slightly embarrassed one or two of the senior members.

Britain halving the series as they did surprised a great many people; I like to think the reason why we were more successful than previous Ryder Cup teams, and this might sound a little selfish, even big-headed, was because I handled the team in a fashion in which it has never been handled before. I didn't get the team to do any special training or anything like that, I just told them not to change their normal routine. I wanted them to act as if it was just another tournament. I wanted a relaxed team, a confident team and above all, a team in fighting form. Yes, I gave them a bit of a pep talk too.

The finest moment in my golfing life was certainly when all the team stood up at dinner after the Tournament and applauded me. It was a wonderful feeling, and highly gratifying to know that the team was that much behind me.

I believe Britain's performance at Royal Birkdale will have a tremendous effect on the future golf in Britain. I think it will give a big boost to professional golf, amateur golf, in fact all classes of golf. It will act as a wonderful tonic all round.

One of my fondest memories of the match was the magnificent gesture by Leo Fraser, president of the U.S. Professional Golfers'

9

Association who handed the golf trophy back. He insisted that the British P.G.A. should hold the Cup for the next twelve months as a token of the first-ever 'dead heat' in these matches. This was a truly remarkable gesture by Leo and one we in this country have to thank him for.

I have no doubt in my mind that this result will stop further suggestions that future Ryder Cup teams to oppose America should contain overseas players in order to even up the battle. This sort of talk has been killed for ever and I am sure that our performance at Royal Birkdale will have ensured the future of The Ryder Cup for all time.

As for our chances in America in two years' time, I am confident that if our younger players carry on improving the way they are we must have an excellent chance of winning.

Thousands of spectators lined the fairways at Royal Birkdale, and millions lived through the excitement of the match on television. Now with the publication of *Dead Heat—The 1969 Ryder Cup Classic* the full story of this historic match can be most enjoyably absorbed at leisure. The author, Paul Trevillion, is an acknowledged expert on the game and I am pleased to write this foreword to his authoritative and lively account of the 1969 Ryder Cup match.

November 1969   ERIC BROWN

INTRODUCTION

THURSDAY, 18TH SEPTEMBER, 1969 was the day Great Britain was to tee off in an effort to end a twelve year Ryder Cup domination by the United States. Britain were the underdogs in the eyes of the world, including those of this country's leading bookmakers who were offering up to 4–1 against Britain recapturing the Ryder Cup.

Both Ryder Cup team captains, Eric Brown of Great Britain and Sam Snead of America, were confident their team would be the one to triumph at Royal Birkdale.

Said Brown, 'We have a beautifully balanced side. Half of them are very experienced and half are keen youngsters who are going to do their best for their country. I am confident we'll give a very good account of ourselves. I think putting is the key and several of our team are putting very well.'

Sam Snead was a little more cautious when speaking of the American team, 'These boys play on all kinds of courses back in America and I expect they'll adjust very well in a day or two.' Snead meant it as a warning; he was not predicting a win for the U.S. side but everybody knew old Sam believed that this would be the eventual outcome.

Ryder Cup captains, Eric Brown (*left*) and Sam Snead (*right*),
have tea together before the Ryder Cup battle commences.

THE RYDER CUP FORMAT

The Ryder Cup is decided over Foursomes, Fourball Foursomes and Singles.

The programme

THURSDAY	MORNING	4–18 HOLES FOURSOMES
SEPTEMBER 18TH	AFTERNOON	4–18 HOLES FOURSOMES
FRIDAY	MORNING	4–18 HOLES FOURBALL FOURSOMES
SEPTEMBER 19TH	AFTERNOON	4–18 HOLES FOURBALL FOURSOMES
SATURDAY	MORNING	8–18 HOLES SINGLES
SEPTEMBER 20TH	AFTERNOON	8–18 HOLES SINGLES

Eric Brown made it clear that he was against the big ball and that he still wished the Ryder Cup match was being played with the small one. But the decision by the British P.G.A. to play the big ball was taken before he was appointed.

Caddy pointer

Alf Fyles, the caddie's spokesman, complained and threatened strike action because the white nylon boiler suits supplied for them to wear did not look attractive enough, and more important, his men would sweat profusely after a few holes. The dispute was quietly settled by the P.G.A. who proved their points were unjustified.

1 THE BRITISH RYDER CUP TEAM 1969

Britain's Ryder Cup selectors Eric Brown, this year's non-playing captain; Dai Rees, a former Cup captain; and Christy O'Connor, leader in the Order of Merit table, created no surprises when they announced the golfers they had selected (Jacklin, Alliss, Bembridge, Caygill, Hunt and Gallacher) to join the top six in the Order of Merit—O'Connor, Huggett, Butler, Barnes, Townsend and Coles.

ERIC BROWN BRITISH RYDER CUP TEAM CAPTAIN

Eric Brown, the firebrand Scot, has a Ryder Cup record which speaks for itself. He played in four matches between 1953 and 1959, and won all his four singles, his most celebrated victory being over Tommy Bolt when Great Britain triumphed at Lindrick in 1957. Brown's pre-match instructions called for courageous golf: he meant to attack from the start.

'Don't play safe but "go for broke" and play for winning birdies' commanded Brown, 'never leave a putt short, even if it means leaving your foursomes partner with four-footers to putt back. Stay firm and play like hell in the crises.'

'We can beat the Yanks if we play to our full capacity', was Brown's pre-match forecast.

PETER ALLISS

Born in Berlin in 1931, Alliss is the famous son of a famous father
—Percy Alliss—the only father-and-son combination ever to have
played in the Ryder Cup. In 1953, at the early age of 22, Alliss
made his first Ryder Cup appearance and in the same year won
his first tournament.

A brilliant last round 66 which included an outward half of 30
meant Alliss finished in eighth place in the Open Championship
at Royal Lytham this year. The following week he won his first
tournament in Britain for two years when he beat Scotland's
George Will at the 37th hole in the final of the Piccadilly medal.

Alliss has an impressive Ryder Cup record having won ten and
halved four of his Ryder Cup encounters. He has beaten, among
others, Palmer, Casper and Venturi, all U.S. Open Champions
and Gay Brewer, U.S. Masters winner.

16

BRIAN BARNES

Brian Barnes, educated at Millfield Public School, is the son-in-law of former Open Champion Max Faulkner. Standing over six feet and weighing over fourteen stone, Barnes is the giant of the British team. He is also the longest driver in the side, if not in Great Britain.

His first major tournament win came with the Agfacolor Film Tournament at Stoke Poges in this, the Ryder Cup year. Barnes' victory came at an appropriate time for a psychological barrier about winning was beginning to build up. For two years he had threatened to win on many occasions, only to fall at the last hurdle. Barnes followed up with win number two in a Coca-Cola Young Professionals event.

Twenty-four-year-old Barnes is one of the five newcomers to the British Ryder Cup team.

MAURICE BEMBRIDGE

Internationally golf-minded Maurice Bembridge is a regular overseas traveller during the winter months. He is convinced that the
experience gained in South Africa, Australia and the Far East has
helped him to establish himself in the top ranks of British golf.

Bembridge, a 24-year-old Ryder Cup new boy from Little
Aston, scored his first major solo victory when he won the *News
of the World* match-play Championship beating 56-year-old Dai
Rees by 6 and 5 in the final.

'I always wanted to be in the Ryder Cup,' admitted Bembridge,
'it was one of the first things I had in mind and I am very grateful
to be in it this year.'

Last winter he retained the Kenya Open title and with Angel
Gallardo he won the Sumrie Tournament. He was in twelfth
position in the Order of Merit at the time of selection.

PETER BUTLER

The cool calculating 37-year-old Peter Butler is one of the most respected tournament players. He is a model for all golfers who prefer the delicate touch as against the power game.

He represents the Harbourne Club in his native Birmingham and also the St. Cloud club in Paris. In August this year Butler had an impressive victory in the RTV Rentals Tournament at Little Ireland, Cork. On winning, Butler paid tribute to his lucky putter which he picked up in Bombay and with which he won his first major tournament ten years ago, Butler finished one stroke behind Brian Huggett and Tony Grubb in the Bowmaker, and was runner-up in the Dunlop Masters.

This was Butler's second Ryder Cup match: he previously played at Royal Birkdale in 1965 but with little success. He lost three and halved two of his games.

ALEX CAYGILL

Twenty-nine-year-old Caygill won the British Youth Championship in 1960 and 1962: he then turned professional and won the
Assistants title and Rediffusion event in 1963.

Unfortunately Caygill, plagued by nerves, developed stomach
ulcers and faded from the tournament scene. It was not until 1969
that he returned to winning form when he won the Penfold
Tournament at Hill Barn, Worthing. In the Martini Tournament
at Bournemouth he shared the leading place with Graham
Henning of South Africa.

Over the year, Caygill has displayed a fighting heart and great
courage when winning, proving conclusively that he has overcome
the nervousness which at one time seriously threatened his career.

NEIL COLES

Since 1961, Neil Coles has been one of Great Britain's most consistent performers in the Ryder Cup competition. In fact, consistency has been the hallmark of Coles' game over the years and he has proved himself a great golfer under pressure.

Although Coles is without a major tournament win this year, he has been, need we say, extremely consistent throughout. Partnered by his Ryder Cup colleague Bernard Hunt, he tied for third place in the Sumrie Tournament at Pannal. He was joint fourth at the Agfacolor Film Tournament, joint fifth in the Bowmaker ·and joint sixth at the Martini, Daks and Penfold events.

At the age of 34, Neil Coles was selected for his fifth consecutive Ryder Cup match to be played on one of his favourite courses— Royal Birkdale.

BERNARD GALLACHER

A slim, dark, good-looking youngster with a choirboy face which masks a ruthless determination to achieve golf perfection, is 20-year-old Bernard Gallacher, the youngest player ever to represent Great Britain in the Ryder Cup matches.

Born at Bathgate, Scotland, Gallacher broke eleven course records before turning professional. Strangely enough for one so young he is one of the game's deepest thinkers, a most thorough student of the tactical play in golf.

A sensational three-week run during May and June in this Ryder Cup year saw Gallacher win the Schweppes Tournament and finish runner-up to Brian Barnes in the Agfacolor Film Tournament and runner-up to Brian Huggett in the Daks. He had his second tournament success of the season when he won the Wills' Open.

BRIAN HUGGETT

Thirty-two-year-old Brian Huggett, nicknamed the 'Welsh Bull-
dog' because of his tenacity and courage under fire is making
his third appearance in the Ryder Cup matches.

In 1968 Huggett reshaped his swing in order to cope with the
big ball experiment which was in force for all P.G.A. Tournaments. It proved a profitable adjustment for he went on to win the
Sumrie Tournament, the Martini and the *News of the World*
Match-Play Championship.

Huggett's good form has stayed with him throughout 1969.
With victory in the Daks and a tie for first in the Bowmaker
Tournament, he was also a semi-finalist in the *News of the World*
Match-Play.

BERNARD HUNT

Although without a tournament win in this country in 1969, 39-year-old Bernard Hunt's consistent play and vast experience has earned him a Ryder Cup place. He will be making his eighth appearance for Great Britain in these biennial Ryder Cup clashes.

Hunt started the year in sparkling form on the Continent by winning the Algarve Open at Penina in March and the Italian BP Tournament at Olgiata a fortnight later. In Ireland he was joint second in both the Gallaher Ulster and the RTV International. He also finished joint third when partnered by Ryder Cup colleague Neil Coles in the Sumrie Fourball. He was joint fourth in the Schweppes Tournament, joint fifth in the Bowmaker and Carroll's International and joint sixth in the Martini.

He made his Ryder Cup debut in 1953, was not selected for the 1955 match, but has played in every one since.

TONY JACKLIN

At 13 years of age Jacklin won his first title, the Lincolnshire
Boys' Championship and he went on to retain the title for the
next three years. Eleven years later at the age of 24, Tony Jacklin
shook the world when he won the Jacksonville Open in Florida
just a few short months after joining the American circuit. In
doing so he became the first British golfer to win a major tournament in the States since Ted Ray performed the feat in 1920.

In July of this year at Royal Lytham & St. Annes, he went one
better when he became the first Briton to win the Open Championship since Max Faulkner took the trophy in 1951.

Jacklin, a former newspaper delivery boy and son of a Scun-
thorpe lorry driver, played in the 1967 Ryder Cup match in
America; he won two, lost three and halved one of the six games
he played.

CHRISTY O'CONNOR

Forty-four-year-old Christy O'Connor has had an uninterrupted run in Ryder Cup matches since 1955.

In the Open Championship at Royal Lytham this year Christy O'Connor had the lowest single round for the Championship when he scored 65 in the second round. He eventually finished fifth.

O'Connor, a veteran in terms of Ryder Cup experience is playing in his eighth consecutive match. In his previous appearances he has won seven, lost fifteen and halved one. Only Peter Alliss of the seven British players who have previously played in the Ryder Cup, has won more games.

O'Connor qualified for his Ryder Cup place by topping the Order of Merit. He won the Gallaher Ulster in Belfast and was runner-up to Alex Caygill in the Penfold Tournament, and joint third in the Carroll's International and Dunlop Masters.

PETER TOWNSEND

Twenty-two-year-old Peter Townsend from Porters Park Golf
Club had an outstanding amateur record in which he represented
Britain in the Walker Cup. He turned professional in 1966 and
after an unhappy start in which he remodelled his swing, he won
the 1967 Dutch Open for his first professional tournament success.

In the past couple of years he has played mainly in America
but in the space of a few weeks in this country last year, he
became the leading money winner totalling over £9,000. He won
the Coca-cola Young Professionals Tournament, the Piccadilly
P.G.A. Close Championship and was runner-up in the Alcan
Golfer of the Year Championship played at Royal Birkdale.

Earlier this year Townsend had his U.S.P.G.A. playing ticket
taken away, only to have it returned. His performances in America
since then have been good, if not spectacular.

2 THE UNITED STATES RYDER CUP TEAM 1969

The selection of the American Ryder Cup team was based on points gained after the 1968 P.G.A. Championship and not, as formerly, on an accumulation of points over the two full years between each Ryder Cup set-to. This meant the U.S. team fielded the twelve most successful players during the year preceding the match. It turned out to be an exceptionally strong team: although many of them were unknown in this country, their records made impressive readings. Between them they had won over 130 titles on the American tour and five of them, Nicklaus, Casper, Littler, Trevino and Floyd, had lifted major U.S. titles.

SAM SNEAD THE UNITED STATES RYDER CUP TEAM CAPTAIN

For Sam Snead, this match was something of a sentimental journey, for it was at Southport and Ainsdale, very near to where this year's Ryder Cup took place, that he made his debut as a Ryder Cup player way back in 1937.

This was the first occasion that the American team won in this country and the Americans have won every match that has since been played in Britain with the exception of Lindrick in 1957.

Fifty-seven-year-old Sam Snead, who played in nine Ryder Cup teams spanning the years 1937–59 and who won our British Open at St. Andrews in 1946, has considerable experience of the golfing conditions in this country.

TOMMY AARON

Tommy Aaron is rated one of the greatest stylists in golf, a smooth easy rhythm enables him to hit his shots with an authoritative ease.

Aaron, who at one time early in his career, looked as if he might become an American football player, earned his class 'A' U.S.P.G.A. membership in 1967 to become eligible to compete for the first time in the Ryder Cup this year.

A former Walker Cup player, thirty-two-year-old Tommy Aaron, from Callaway Gardens, Georgia, was nine years on the U.S.P.G.A. tour before he registered his first win when he beat Sam Snead in a play-off to become the Canadian Open Champion.

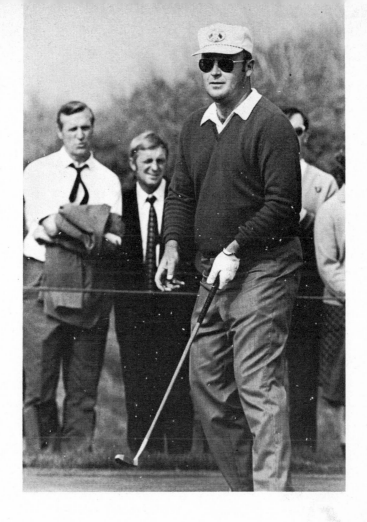

MILLER BARBER

The thirty-eight-year-old bachelor Miller Barber is said to have a swing that would make a week-ender blush: even so Barber, who owns his own golf course in Sherman, Texas, hammers out a great living with it.

Barber, who wears huge sunglasses regardless of the weather, has created a certain amount of mystery about himself for he does not fraternise with fellow golf pros. Because of this he is affectionately known on the tour as the 'Mysterious Mr. X'.

This year he won the rain-curtailed Kaiser International and finished in the top ten in all four of the world's major championships—the British and U.S. Opens, the Masters and U.S.P.G.A. Championship.

This was Barber's first appearance in the Ryder Cup matches.

FRANK BEARD

Frank Beard comes from a sporting background: his father is a former golf professional and his half-brother Ralph was a former all-American baseball star. Beard, a dedicated visitor to the practice tee, treats golf like an office job, his hours are nine till five.

In 1964 Beard contracted encephalitis and was in a coma for three days. His condition was so serious he was administered the last rites of the Catholic Church. But against the odds, Beard recovered and even more surprisingly he was back on the Tour later that year. But when nominated for the Ben Hogan Trophy for the golfer who has overcome the greatest adversity, Beard declined. 'I didn't do anything', he said, 'I just got well'. This was Beard's first appearance in the Ryder Cup matches.

BILLY CASPER

Billy Casper, who has twice won the U.S. Open Championship, is rated one of the finest putters in golf today, and is also rated one of the nicest personalities. Casper, of the Mormon faith, is a deeply religious man who accepts both victory and defeat in the same quiet, modest manner.

Casper enjoys playing golf in this country because he finds he is not attacked by so many allergies. Pesticides and sprays used on the courses in the States affect him badly.

Casper, who has been known to eat buffalo steaks as part of an unusual diet, has a great deal of Ryder Cup experience. He has represented his country in every Ryder Cup match since 1961.

DALE DOUGLASS

Thirty-three-year-old Dale Douglass, who insists he is one of those colourless players who 'fades into the landscape', won his first tournament this year when he walked off with the first prize in the Azalea Open at Wilmington, North Carolina. This was a 'satellite' tournament played concurrently with the Tournament of Champions in Las Vegas, and another smaller event in Tallahassee, Florida. In June, Douglass won the Kemper Open against a top-class field to prove emphatically that he had truly arrived.

Although Dale Douglass is not well known over here he has been playing the American Tour since 1960, admittedly with only modest success. Lanky Douglass who has a very upright swing which resembles that of the other tall golfer, Masters Champion George Archer, is an excellent striker of the ball.

RAYMOND FLOYD

Twenty-seven-year-old Ray Floyd, who stands over six feet and weighs over 200 lbs., looked at one time to be heading for a career in baseball. But victory in the 1961 International Junior Chamber of Commerce Championship convinced Floyd that his future lay in golf.

As a youngster of 20, he won his first Tour victory at St. Petersburg, Florida in 1963, the same year he won the Golf Digest magazine 'Rookie of the Year' award.

He had to wait two years for his next victory at St. Pauls, Minnesota and then an even longer wait of four years before he won again when he succeeded Tony Jacklin as the Jacksonville Open Champion.

After winning the American Classic he put the seal on a truly great year by winning the American P.G.A. Championship. This was Floyd's first appearance in Ryder Cup matches.

DAVE HILL

Thirty-two-year-old Dave Hill is slightly built, stands just under six feet and looks remarkably like our own Peter Townsend. Hill's reputation is built on a hot putter and an even hotter temper. He has twice been censored in America for flashes of temper.

A native of Michigan, he has been a touring pro since 1959. He first began to attract attention in 1967 when he won the Memphis Open and ended the season with a total of almost $50,000.

This year he repeated his Memphis Open triumph and followed up by taking the Buick Open. He made it three wins when he headed the field in the Philadelphia Classic, these wins alone totalled $37,000.

This was Hill's first Ryder Cup appearance.

GENE LITTLER

Gene Littler has represented the United States every year since 1961. Having played in four Ryder Cup teams, he and Casper are the two most experienced members of this year's Ryder Cup team.

Littler, of La Jolla, California, turned pro soon after winning the National Amateur in 1953 but he had to wait until 1961 for his first major title—the U.S. Open. This year he has won two tournaments—the Phoenix Open and the Greater Greensboro Open.

Thirty-seven-year-old Littler is an antique car enthusiast. At the time of writing he owns five, one of which is a pre-war Rolls-Royce.

JACK NICKLAUS

Jack Nicklaus' first tournament victory was the 1962 U.S. Open and to win it he had to defeat Arnold Palmer in a play-off. The emphasis in golf is on the four major championships—the Masters, the U.S. Open, the British Open and the U.S.P.G.A. Nicklaus has won all four, in fact he has a total of seven victories in these events.

Nicklaus, rated the longest and straightest driver in world golf has won only one tournament this year—the Andy Williams Open, way back in January. Admittedly millionaire Jack is not in need of money, but he does need to win another major championship soon if he is to justify the title of the 'greatest golfer in the world today'.

This was Nicklaus' first year of eligibility for Ryder Cup competition.

DAN SIKES

Thirty-eight-year-old Dan Sikes of Jacksonville, Florida gained his Law Degree at the University of Florida. This was quite an achievement for at the time he was playing a great deal of golf. Honour satisfied, Dan decided against going into practice: instead he became a professional golfer.

Today he admits he hates the pressures of the Tour and would love to quit and go back to practising law, but with winnings of $250,000 he simply cannot afford to give up the game.

In 1968 Sikes won the Florida Citrus Open and the Minnesota Classic but this year he has failed to win a tournament. Nevertheless he has put in many fine performances which have enabled him to add to his already considerable bank balance and keep all thoughts of practising at the bar till a later date.

This was Dan Sikes first appearance in Ryder Cup matches.

KEN STILL

Ken Still is an outgoing character who thinks nothing of shouting across three fairways to encourage a friend. He is also a bachelor who will take time off to kiss a pretty girl in the gallery. But way back in 1953 when Still started the Tour, things were far different: he shut the door on his natural enthusiasm and played with a clinical seriousness and the results were bad. In despair he left the game more than a dozen times, always to return. Then came the day he decided to play it for 'laughs' and things improved in a big way. Even so it was not until 1969 that he recorded his first win—the Florida Citrus Open.

Thirty-four-year-old Ken Still's first ambition was to be a base-ball player and he still is a very keen baseball fan today. At one time he aimed to wear a 'Dodger' uniform playing on tour, but the American P.G.A. refused to sanction this.

LEE TREVINO

In 1967 in his first year on the American circuit, Lee Trevino finished fifth in the American Open Championship. The following year, against all the odds, he won the Championship with a record score of 275 which equalled Jack Nicklaus' record. Each of Lee's rounds was under 70.

Born in Dallas, Texas, Lee, who had a spell in the U.S. Marine Corps, is rated the most spectacular one man show that golf has ever known. A natural clown as well as a highly skilful and courageous golfer, his trademark is a dazzling smile and a swing to match.

This year he won the Tucson Open with prize money of $8,333. This was Lee's first Ryder Cup appearance.

Royal Birkdale Golf Club

practice ground

club house

N

S

3 ROYAL BIRKDALE HOLE BY HOLE

The Royal Birkdale golf course, although considered one of the fairest tests in Britain, is a particularly difficult course to master on account of the level of the 'reme' water which lies just below the surface. This helps to produce on this typical seaside course an abundance of humps and hollows. Here a golfer can expect, and will indeed get, many unusual bounces and experience a wind which can spring from a gentle breeze to a blustery wind in the space of a few holes. When the wind blows the golfer who hits his shot low has a distinct advantage for he can cheat the elements by sending his ball below the line of the sandhills.

This magnificent stretch of turf has witnessed many great championships, dramas and the like, during its long and colourful history. Peter Thompson won two of his five British Open Championships here; and Arnold Palmer hit the greatest recovery shot ever seen in golf when he hammered his ball out of a bush on the 16th hole—the old 15th—and braked it a few feet from the pin.

With its many mountainous sandhills which form natural spectator grandstands, Royal Birkdale is the sort of course which once seen, presents the kind of challenge few golfers can resist.

THE CARD OF THE COURSE

Hole	Yards	Par	Hole	Yards	Par
1	493	5	10	393	4
2	427	4	11	412	4
3	416	4	12	190	3
4	212	3	13	517	5
5	358	4	14	202	3
6	533	5	15	536	5
7	158	3	16	401	4
8	459	4	17	510	5
9	410	4	18	513	5
Out	3466	36	In	3674	38

TOTAL 7140 yards   Par: 74

HOLE 1 493 YARDS—PAR 5

With out-of-bounds on the right and a protruding sandbank on
the left, you must hit a straight drive which slightly favours the
left-hand side of the fairway. The many sand traps around the
green do not make the long second shot an easy one.
Caution note: When taking the left route from the tee, take care
not to finish too near the protruding sandbank or difficulties will
arise when attempting to clear with the second shot.

HOLE 2 427 YARDS—PAR 4

Here the left-hand side of the fairway gives you the best line to
the hole. A 4-wood or medium iron for your second shot
(depending on the wind) makes this a fairly comfortable par 4.
With an east wind at your back the second shot for the likes of
Nicklaus could be as little as a wedge.

HOLE 3 416 YARDS—PAR 4

A steep sand dune protrudes from the right just in front of the
green so your tee shot must be aimed to the left-hand side of the
fairway to open up the hole. Once again, depending on the wind,
your second shot should not be too demanding.

HOLE 1

HOLE 2

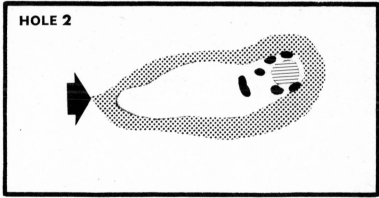

HOLE 3

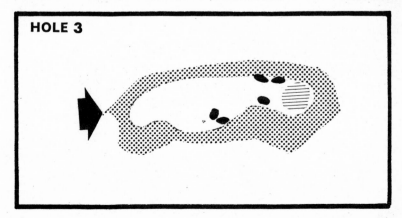

HOLE 4 212 YARDS—PAR 3

This is the first of the short holes and the green, which is low, is considered the heaviest on the course. So although it is well bunkered you can pitch onto it with safety. Because of the extreme wetness the ball will not roll on to the green, but it enables it to hold a shot hit with a driver.

HOLE 5 358 YARDS—PAR 4

There is a lake on the right but this doesn't really come into play. The best line to the hole is up the left-hand side of the fairway with a lofted iron for your second. On a really calm day a long hitter can carry the right-hand mound, but he will not see the end result of his tee shot.

HOLE 6 533 YARDS—PAR 5

From the newly built back tee you require two enormous shots to reach the green, the second of which has to be played over high ground which divides the fairway. The line for the tee shot should favour the right-hand side of the bunker which divides the fairway.

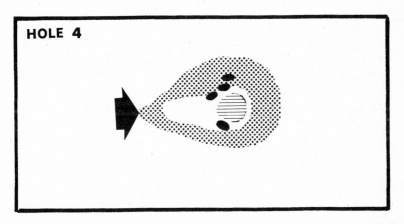

HOLE 4

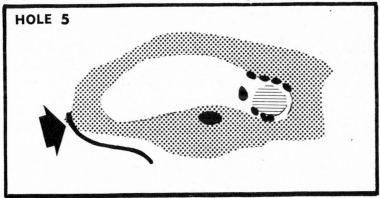

HOLE 5

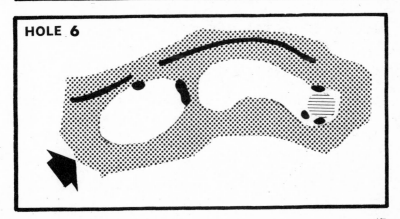

HOLE 6

HOLE 7   158 YARDS—PAR 3

This shot is played from an elevated tee, the back of which is sheltered from the wind. When in doubt, always test for wind strength at the front of the tee.

HOLE 8   459 YARDS—PAR 4

This hole which is played from a raised tee, and has the sea behind it, has a slight dog-leg to the left. It means a carefully placed drive favouring the left to avoid the right-hand side of a fairway dotted with bunkers.

HOLE 9   410 YARDS—PAR 4

From the tee it is wise not to be too far left for it is very easy to run into trouble. Your second shot is to a raised green with the clubhouse close by. If you must get a par four to win, a 1-iron or 3-wood off the tee is advisable in order to avoid the bunker on the right.

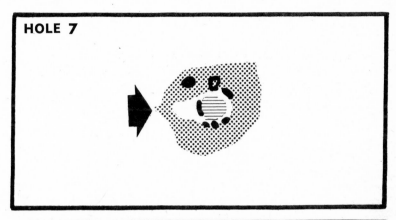

HOLE 7

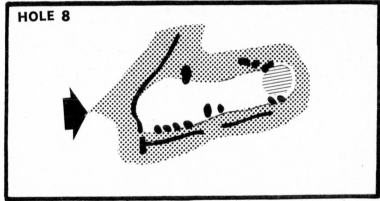

HOLE 8

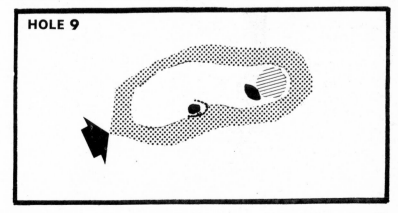

HOLE 9

HOLE 10 393 YARDS—PAR 4

The sloping fairway will manoeuvre your ball to the right on this
sharp left-hand dog-leg. A reasonable tee shot will leave you at the
corner of the dog-leg, setting you up for your second shot to the
green.

HOLE 11 412 YARDS—PAR 4

An extra long tee shot is required here in order to make your
approach shot to the green a relatively simple one, for this is the
most difficult green on the course. It narrows towards the back—
the most likely spot for the hole to be cut.

HOLE 12 190 YARDS—PAR 3

A straightforward par 3. You hit your tee shot across a valley to a
green guarded by high sand dunes. Aim slightly to the left side of
the green: a 5 is possible if you miss on the right and land in
really bad rough.

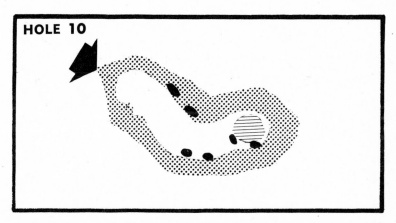

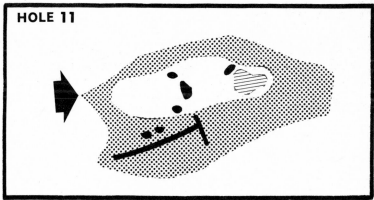

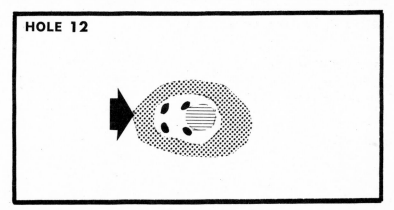

HOLE 13   517 YARDS—PAR 5

Care must be taken when lining up because of the off-set tee position. Aim for cross bunker on fairway. A long accurate drive up the right-hand side of the fairway will leave you an equally long second shot if you are to hit the green in two for a possible birdie.

HOLE 14   202 YARDS—PAR 3

Like the par 3, seventh hole, here again you have to test for wind strength at the front of the tee. Always a difficult shot (more so in the wind) to a well bunkered green.

HOLE 15   536 YARDS—PAR 5

The longest hole on the course, demanding a long drive to a very narrow fairway. A wooden second shot which has to carry eight bunkers will leave you near enough to wedge or pitch on to a green that slopes slightly upwards.

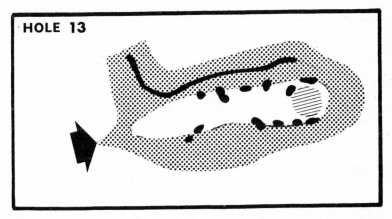

HOLE 13

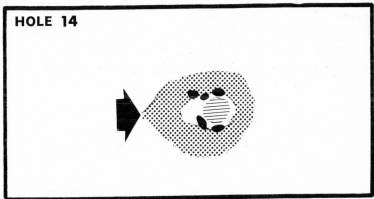

HOLE 14

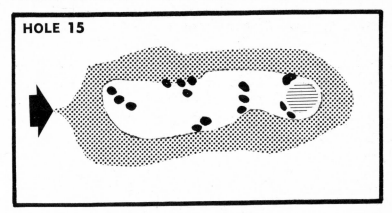

HOLE 15

HOLE 16   401 YARDS—PAR 4

One of the widest fairways on the course enabling you to attack
from the tee. A drive of 260 yards will leave you with a 4-or
an 8-iron approach shot (depending on the wind). In the deep
rough by the two bunkers on the right of the fairway there is a
plaque commemorating Arnold Palmer's remarkable mid-iron
shot to the green in the 1961 Open. The hole was then the 15th,
but it has since been re-designed and lengthened. Keep well away
from this plaque which is not the route to the green.

HOLE 17   501 YARDS—PAR 5

Here your tee shot has to be driven straight over the edge of the
hill on the right with a driver. Manoeuvre this safely and you are
left with a straightforward second shot to a green which is
heavily bunkered.

HOLE 18   513 YARDS—PAR 5

This hole which has been stretched back to 513 yards with a tee
set to the right, needs a really long tee shot to be sure of
clearing the two bunkers up the fairway. Second shot requires a
3-iron or a 3-wood depending on the wind. Once again, there is
bunker trouble all round the green demanding an accurate
second shot. Tee shot should just clear right-hand end of bunker
on right to make sure of avoiding the threatening bunker on the
left.
The Professional at Royal Birkdale, Robert Halsall who has been
associated with the club for forty years, expertly sums up the
course: 'Royal Birkdale provides an exciting challenge; it
demands great length and accuracy and many of the greens are
approached over flat bare ground which makes judgement of
distance for your second shot difficult. The wind can alter from
hour to hour which means it requires a great deal of experience to
play the course well.'

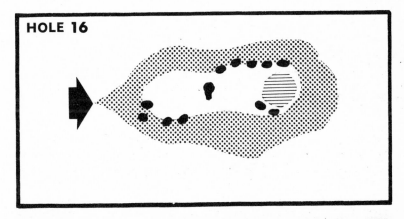

HOLE 16

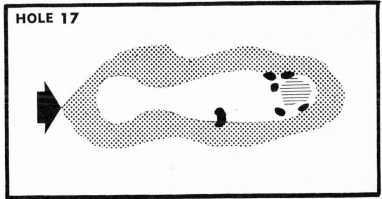

HOLE 17

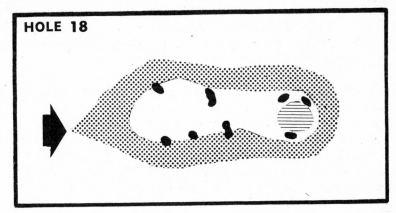

HOLE 18

4 FIRST DAY FOURSOMES

MORNING

When the flags of the two great Nations were run up on the morning of the first day without so much as a ripple, it was clear to all that Birkdale was without the feared menace of a blustery wind. The opening ceremony was a moving and emotional experience for both the players and the spectators alike. The pulse beat a little faster and the heart swelled with a little surge of pride, just as Leo Fraser, President of the Professional Golfers' Association of America, had predicted.

Eric Brown, the British Ryder Cup captain, fielded his strongest eight for the morning battle. He gave the key No. 1 and No. 4 positions to tried, experienced pairs (Coles-Huggett, O'Connor-Alliss). The two middle places went to Jacklin and three youngsters making their first Ryder Cup appearances (Jacklin-Townsend, Bembridge-Gallacher).

The most exciting match of the morning play featured Bernard Gallacher and Maurice Bembridge who faced the Mexican Lee Trevino and baseball fan Ken Still. The Americans, with three single putts on each of the first three greens, got off to a blistering 4 3 3 start and Great Britain found themselves 2 down. Nobody, not even these two Americans, could keep that sort of super golf up and reality was restored when they three-putted the short 4th and allowed Gallacher and Bembridge to take a valuable hole back. At the turn the match was all square, both pairs having gone out in 34. On the inward stretch the British youngsters played by far the better golf. They birdied the 10th when Gallacher holed a four-yarder to go 1 up, and went 2 up at the 13th. Here Still was struck by his own ball playing a sand shot. Although they lost the long 536 yards 15th to a birdie, they won the match on the long 17th when they knocked in a birdie putt.

There was now a very optimistic feeling in the air. Britain were 2 up for Neil Coles and Brian Huggett had hammered the top American pair, Floyd and Barber 3 and 2 in the first match.

Ryder Cup captain Eric Brown with Tom Haliburton raced round the course in an electric buggie encouraging and informing his boys of the overall progress. Dai Rees, a member of the Ryder Cup committee, seemed to be everywhere. Whenever a ball found the rough or a talking point arose, Rees was on hand.

56

Ryder Cup captain Eric Brown with Tom Haliburton raced round the course in an electric buggie, encouraging and informing his team of the overall match progress.

Ray Floyd explodes out of a bunker. Floyd and his partner Miller
Barber had an unhappy start to the Ryder Cup for Neil Coles and
Brian Huggett beat them 3 and 2.

Neil Coles putts from off the fringe at the back of the green.
Huggett and Coles won the opening match for Great Britain when
they beat Miller Barber and Ray Floyd 3 and 2.

Opposite: Dave Hill charges home a birdie putt during foursomes against Jacklin and Townsend.

Below: Dave Hill celebrates after holing out by throwing his putter in the air but the celebrations ended there. He and Aaron (*left*) lost their foursomes to Jacklin and Townsend by 3 and 1.

Open champion Jacklin and Peter Townsend were quickly 2 up in their match with birdies in the first three holes. They kept this margin intact until the 10th when the Americans Hill and Aaron pulled one back. But that was the last time the Americans looked like making a fight of it for the British pair won the 14th with a 4 to a 6 and then an eagle 3 on the 17th which was set up by a magnificent Townsend 3-wood to the green. This was good enough for Great Britain to win the match 3 and 1.

The delighted crowd was now racing over the sand dunes, searching out the best vantage points in an effort to see more of the final match. As one course steward explained, 'You can always

tell the state of the matches by the speed the crowd walk. When
we are doing well, they fairly charge along.'

In the final match of the morning series, Peter Alliss lined up a
putt on the 18th green which was to give Britain a clean sweep
of the morning round and a 4–0 lead. Unfortunately his well
struck putt rimmed the hole and stayed out, allowing Casper and
Frank Beard to halve the match.

It was a sad note to end on but the morning glory still belonged
to Great Britain for they went in to lunch with a $3\frac{1}{2}$–$\frac{1}{2}$ lead.

HOLE	1	2	3	4	5	6	7	8	9	Out	10	11	12	13	14	15	16	17	18	In	Total
YARDS	493	427	416	212	358	533	158	459	410	3466	393	412	190	517	202	536	401	510	513	3674	7140
PAR	5	4	4	3	4	5	3	4	4	36	4	4	3	5	3	5	4	5	5	38	74

Players

	1	2	3	4	5	6	7	8	9	Out	10	11	12	13	14	15	16	17	18	In	Total
Coles–Huggett	5	4	4	4	4	5	3	3	4	36	4	4	3	4	3	–	4				1 under par
Barber–Floyd	5	4	4	3	4	5	3	3	5	36	4	4	3	5	4	o	4				2 over par
G.B. won 3 and 2																					
Gallacher–Bembridge	4	4	4	3	3	5	3	4	4	34	3	4	3	–	3	5	4	4			4 under par
Trevino–Still	4	3	3	4	3	5	3	5	4	34	4	4	3	o	3	4	4	5			2 under par
G.B. won 2 and 1																					
Jacklin–Townsend	4	3	3	3	4	5	3	4	4	33	4	4	3	4	3	4	4	3			7 under par
Hill–Aaron	4	4	4	3	4	5	3	4	4	35	3	4	3	6	3	4	4	5			2 under par
G.B. won 3 and 1																					
O'Connor–Alliss	4	4	5	4	4	4	2	4	4	35	4	4	3	5	2	4	4	5	5	36	3 under par
Casper–Beard	5	4	4	3	4	o	3	4	3	–	4	4	3	4	3	4	4	5	5	36	2 under par
G.B. and U.S. halved																					

GREAT BRITAIN 3, UNITED STATES 0 (one halved)

AFTERNOON FIRST DAY FOURSOMES

American Ryder Cup Captain Sam Snead ruefully admitted that what he had to say to his team over their lunch was unprintable. Whatever it was it had the desired effect, for the Americans, fearful of their reputation, teed off in the afternoon determined to win back the lost ground.

In the first match Hill and Aaron—who had tasted defeat in the morning—beat Coles and Huggett on the 18th when Hill knocked in a 5-foot birdie putt after a close, tense struggle. Hill's winning putt actually ran round the cup and stopped on the far edge for a second before toppling back in.

Gallacher and Bembridge, the heroes of the morning round, hung on bravely against Trevino and Littler, but it was in vain. The Americans, in a match in which holes exchanged hands freely, birdied the 18th, where Gallacher drove into the rough, for a two-hole victory.

Only Jacklin and Townsend were able to win a second point when they edged out Casper and Beard by one hole on the 18th. In this match Billy Casper jarred his right hand when playing from the rough at the 13th, 'The ball was in half an old divot mark', explained Casper, 'the previous guy had stopped on the shot and I tried to follow through.' But Jacklin believed the turning point in this match was on the previous hole—the 12th—when Casper missed a holeable putt for a 2 which would have put America 2 up. As it was Britain squared the match at the very next hole where the Americans took 6. After the match Casper refused to blame their defeat on his injured hand, but it's fair to say that he did hit two un-Casper-like hooked tee shots at the 15th and 17th holes, which, to say the least, did not help their chances.

Inside the ropes, following the Jacklin-Townsend, Casper-Beard match in the afternoon, were the respective player's wives. Patti Beard in a mini skirt, red tights and high black boots looked delightful; Townsend's wife Lorna looked a dazzling picture with her long blond hair, flowing behind her. Vivien Jacklin, expecting a happy event in late autumn, looked equally charming in a beautifully tailored cape-coat. The attractive Mrs. Casper in a

64

Foot trouble for Jacklin at the first hole during his foursomes battle with Casper and Beard. After applying band-aid, Jacklin replaced his sock and shoe to the amusement of the crowd.

Glamour and the latest fashion was in evidence on the course during the afternoon round. Here four wives watch their husbands in action. (*Left to right*) Lorna Townsend, Patti Beard, Vivien Jacklin and Shirley Casper.

67

checked three-quarter length suit and high white boots, completed
the colourful quartet.

The old firm of Butler and Hunt went down on the last green to
Nicklaus and Sikes. After a bad Nicklaus tee shot which found the
rough on the left, Sikes was able to hammer the ball out near
enough to the green for Nicklaus to wedge to two feet for a vital

Townsend plays out of a bunker watched by partner Tony Jacklin during foursome match in which they beat Casper and Beard 1 up.

birdie putt. Hunt's 25-foot putt to match it, died two inches wide of the hole—a brave but unprofitable try.

Thanks to Tony Jacklin and Peter Townsend's double, Britain ended the day with a 4–3 lead with one halved. Said the two British heroes, 'We played well together, it was just one of those good days and we enjoyed it'; laughed Jacklin, 'I got a bit tired this

Bernard Hunt successfully splashing out from a bunker.

afternoon, but we pulled ourselves together over the last few holes.'
Peter Townsend chipped into the conversation with 'At the par 5's
we hit the better tee shots and set ourselves up for more birdies
than they did.'

The two Ryder Cup captains had different stories to tell. Eric
Brown with a broad grin on his face, told all within earshot, 'We
went in as the underdogs and we've come out ahead: there were
two matches we could have won if we had got the run of the ball.'
Sam Snead, with a smile which was unable to disguise the worried

Dan Sikes moves an awful lot of sand and gets the ball safely out of a bunker. Jack Nicklaus and Dan Sikes won their afternoon foursomes match against Hunt and Butler by one hole.

furrows in his brow, simply said, 'I'm happy Britain are not leading by more and there is no need to say how I felt about the morning play; I think my boys will get more accustomed to the course and play better, especially in the mornings.'

Neil Coles and Brian Huggett had landed the day's biggest

FIRST DAY—FOURSOMES *Afternoon*

HOLE	1	2	3	4	5	6	7	8	9	Out	10	11	12	13	14	15	16	17	18	In	Total
YARDS	493	427	416	212	358	533	158	459	410	3466	393	412	190	517	202	536	401	510	513	3674	7140
PAR	5	4	4	3	4	5	3	4	4	36	4	4	3	5	3	5	4	5	5	38	74

Players

	1	2	3	4	5	6	7	8	9	Out	10	11	12	13	14	15	16	17	18	In	Total
Coles-Huggett	5	5	3	3	5	5	3	5	4	38	3	4	3	5	3	6	3	5	5	37	1 over par
Hill-Aaron	6	5	4	3	4	5	2	4	3	36	4	4	3	5	3	7	3	5	4	38	level par
U.S. won 1 hole																					
Gallacher-Bembridge	4	4	4	3	3	5	3	5	4	35	4	4	4	—	4	5	4	4	5	—	level par
Trevino-Littler	4	4	4	3	4	4	2	4	4	33	4	5	3	○	3	5	4	5	4	—	2 under par
U.S. won 2 holes																					
Jacklin-Townsend	4	4	4	4	4	4	4	4	3	35	4	5	3	5	3	5	4	4	4	37	2 under par
Casper-Beard	4	4	4	3	4	5	3	4	○	—	4	4	3	6	3	5	4	5	4	38	level par
G.B. won 1 hole																					
Hunt-Butler	4	6	3	4	4	5	3	4	4	37	4	4	3	4	3	5	4	6	5	38	1 over par
Nicklaus-Sikes	4	4	5	3	4	5	3	4	4	36	4	4	3	4	3	5	5	6	4	38	level par
U.S. won 1 hole																					

GREAT BRITAIN 1, UNITED STATES 3.

DAY ONE—OVERALL TOTAL—GREAT BRITAIN 4, UNITED STATES 3 (one halved)

72

victory margin against Miller Barber and Ray Floyd; they won the 13th, 14th and 15th in a row for a 3 and 2 victory.

Possibly the shot of the day was Townsend's exquisite pitch over the edge of the bunker on the right of the 18th green which stopped less than six inches from the hole for a conceded putt. This meant the two British lads had got round in one under par and earned a two holes victory over Casper and Beard.

On the first day the British lion had roared and showed it had teeth, but there were still two more days and a lot of golf to come.

Strategy pointer

In the 1965 match at Royal Birkdale, a plan to beat the Americans by placing the pins in tight positions behind bunkers, rebounded on the British team because the Americans had had more experience of attacking tight pin placements. This year the pins were, in general, placed in the back centre of the green which as Ryder Cup committee member, Dai Rees, explained 'enabled the British players to play their normal pitch and run game.' This meant the high-flying, fast-stopping, back-spinning approach shots favoured by the Americans did not gain an unfair advantage. 'Although it was the same for both teams,' went on Rees, 'it had a more settling effect on the British players.'

5 SECOND DAY FOURBALLS

MORNING

In the fourball matches on the second day, Brown paired experienced players with Ryder Cup newcomers, splitting the successful pairing of the previous day—Jacklin and Townsend.

A warm sun and little wind meant ideal conditions as the first of the fourball foursomes stepped onto the tee. Townsend was partnered by O'Connor in the opening match and they were off to a great start, both picking up birdie 4's on the first green to take the lead over their American opponents Hill and Douglass.

They halved the 2nd but America brought it back to all square at the 3rd. It didn't stay that way for long, for on the 212 yards par-3 4th, O'Connor holed a 50-foot putt for a 2 to restore the home team's lead. The Americans refused to be rattled by this and hit back at the 6th hole where Douglass sank a five-foot birdie to level the match.

They reached the turn in 35, all square. Then Great Britain went 1 up when O'Connor slotted in a five-foot putt. But before they could press home their advantage, the short par-3 12th enabled the Americans to level yet again: this time it was Hill's turn to sink a long putt for a birdie 2.

The next hole, the 517 yards par-5 13th allowed Townsend to let fly with two enormous shots to reach the green in two. He finished off the good work by sinking an eagle putt. The huge crowd surrounding the green let out the biggest roar of the day, much to Townsend's delight. Now, surely America must crack, but no, for at the very next hole, the 202 yards par 3, they brought the match back to all square.

Now it was the home team's turn to prove they could fight back and they did when O'Connor won the next hole to put Great Britain in front yet again. The 16th, 17th and 18th holes were halved which was good enough to give Great Britain a one hole victory in a sensational curtain-raiser.

In the second match Huggett and Caygill had a tough battle with Floyd and Barber of America. Caygill chipped into the hole at the 6th for an eagle and Floyd squared the match at the 9th where he holed a 20-foot putt. They reached the turn all square. It stayed that way through the inward nine with no holes chang-

74

Christy O'Connor sparks off a gallery roar as a long putt winds its way over the green into the hole.

ing hands until the 17th, when Caygill holed for a 4 and Floyd
missed his putt from 8 feet, so putting Britain 1 up. Ray Floyd
greeted the 18th hole with two enormous shots to make the
heavily bunkered green with ease. He then rammed home his
12-foot putt for an eagle. The Huggett and Caygill birdie was just
not good enough so the match ended all square.

The third match, Barnes-Alliss against Trevino-Littler saw the
home pair struggling for figures on the outward half. Three down·
at the 7th, they looked in serious trouble and only a magnificent
20-foot winning birdie putt by Brian Barnes at the 9th enabled
Great Britain to turn 2 down.

The 393 yard, par-4 10th presented Barnes with another long
putt for a birdie and he made no mistake. Now the British team
were only 1 down and hope was rising.

Trevino quickly put an end to this with a 20-foot putt across
the 11th green for a birdie and a two hole advantage once again.
At the 13th Barnes and Alliss managed a birdie to cut the deficit
to one hole. At the 15th—the 536-yard par 5, they levelled the
match and the fight was on. The 16th was halved, then Trevino,
with yet another long putt for yet another birdie won the 17th
for the Americans. Both Barnes and Alliss had long putts on the
18th to save the match, but both left them well short. So Great
Britain went down by 1 hole in a thriller.

Still on the course, Jacklin and Neil Coles were playing inspired
golf against Nicklaus and Dan Sikes in this, the last match of the
morning round. Both sides were out in 32, the fifth time this
figure had been recorded at this stage that morning.

The inward half saw Great Britain take the lead at the 10th,
thanks to a Jacklin 3, lose it at the 536-yard 15th and then go back in
the lead at the 17th when Neil Coles holed out.

The 18th hole was halved giving Jacklin and Coles a victory,
and a better ball score of 65—9 under par, over the strong,
possibly the strongest, American pairing of Nicklaus and Sikes.

When the morning round was completed and the scoreboard
registered a 7–5 lead in Great Britain's favour, there was one man
we had to thank—Ryder Cup captain Eric Brown for his inspired
decision to split the Townsend-Jacklin partnership. Both Jacklin
and Townsend played their part in the two matches won by the
home team that morning.

Brian Huggett almost holes out at the 18th in the fourball foursomes match against Floyd and Barber. The match was halved.

Alex Caygill successfully explodes from a trap at the 18th green
during the fourball foursomes against Floyd and Barber.

Overleaf: After the rumpus about British players being initially instructed
not to look for lost balls of Americans, the decision was
reversed. Here, O'Connor (*second left*) and Townsend (*far right*)
help look for the lost ball of Dave Hill (*second right*) during their
fourball foursomes which the home partnership won by one hole.

HOLE	1	2	3	4	5	6	7	8	9	Out	10	11	12	13	14	15	16	17	18	In	Total
YARDS	493	427	416	212	358	533	158	459	410	3466	393	412	190	517	202	536	401	510	513	3674	7140
PAR	5	4	4	3	4	5	3	4	4	36	4	4	3	5	3	5	4	5	5	38	74

SECOND DAY—FOURBALLS *Morning*

Players

	1	2	3	4	5	6	7	8	9	Out	10	11	12	13	14	15	16	17	18	In	Total
O'Connor-Townsend	4	4	5	2	4	5	3	4	4	35	3	4	3	3	4	4	4	4	4	33	6 under par
Hill-Douglass	5	4	4	3	4	4	3	4	4	35	4	4	2	4	3	5	4	4	4	34	5 under par

G.B. won 1 hole

	1	2	3	4	5	6	7	8	9	Out	10	11	12	13	14	15	16	17	18	In	Total
Huggett-Caygill	5	4	3	3	4	3	3	3	4	32	4	4	3	5	3	5	4	4	4	36	6 under par
Floyd-Barber	4	4	4	3	4	4	3	3	3	32	4	4	3	5	3	5	4	5	3	36	6 under par

G.B. and U.S. halved

	1	2	3	4	5	6	7	8	9	Out	10	11	12	13	14	15	16	17	18	In	Total
Barnes-Alliss	4	4	4	3	4	5	3	4	3	34	3	4	3	4	3	4	4	5	4	34	6 under par
Trevino-Littler	4	4	3	3	4	4	2	4	4	32	4	3	3	5	3	5	4	4	4	35	7 under par

U.S. won 1 hole

	1	2	3	4	5	6	7	8	9	Out	10	11	12	13	14	15	16	17	18	In	Total
Jacklin-Coles	5	3	4	3	4	4	2	3	4	32	3	4	3	4	3	5	3	4	4	33	9 under par
Nicklaus-Sikes	4	4	4	2	3	4	3	4	4	32	4	4	3	4	3	4	3	5	4	34	8 under par

G.B. won 1 hole

GREAT BRITAIN 2, UNITED STATES 1 (one halved)

Lee Trevino urges on a birdie putt. Trevino and Littler, in their fourball foursomes match, beat Barnes and Alliss by one hole.

AFTERNOON SECOND DAY FOURBALLS

The fourball games in the morning were such long tedious affairs (stretching to almost five hours) they completely disrupted the day's match planning.

After a quickly taken lunch the afternoon matches started so late it was obvious to officials,. players and spectators alike that darkness might well interfere with play if the pattern of the morning round was to be repeated.

Townsend and Butler, who faced Billy Casper and Frank Beard in the opening match, got off to a bad start losing the first hole. They had to wait until the par-3 4th before they levelled.

At the very next hole they went 1 up then they lost the 6th and won the 7th. Four holes had changed hands alternately and the Townsend-Butler partnership had come out of it with a one hole lead. They then promptly lost the 9th and the turn was reached in 32—all square.

After winning the 10th, Townsend and Butler failed to win another hole whereas the American pair, Casper and Beard, won three of those last eight played for an 8 under par two hole victory.

The overall score was now Great Britain 7, United States 6.

The match following, Hill and Still against Huggett and Gallacher, was played to a chorus of booing, the like of which has never been heard on a golf course before. The target for this booing and jeering was the American visitor Ken Still, a fast talking, quick tempered golfer who had annoyed the crowd by repeatedly stopping and rudely shouting back at them. The trouble which had been smouldering since the very first hole, burst into flame on the 7th green when American Dave Hill putted out of turn and Brian Huggett pointed it out to the referee, David Melville, professional at La Moye, Jersey. This sparked off a heated exchange of words and the Americans, who were two up in the match at this time roared 'What the hell, if you want to win this badly, you can have the hole,' and they walked off to the next tee. The American pair had conceded the hole in a fit of temper when, in fact, they were rightfully entitled to replace the ball which had been wrongly played.

84

The rumpus did not end there for Still, who had by this time lost control of himself, had a go at the referee down the 8th fairway. 'That was a bum decision,' he yelled, 'if Britain wants the Cup this bad—why, they can have it!' Still's voice carried clearly to the watching gallery who responded with shouts, boos and jeers.

Huggett then inflamed matters when he answered Still back; it really looked now as if the argument was going to be settled by fists. Dai Rees, I imagine, was of the same opinion for he intervened in an effort to calm down both Huggett and Still who were now shouting at each other in a threatening manner. At this point the booing of the crowd had reached frightening proportions, one or two had to be restrained from leaping the chestnut fencing. A person next to me brought back his arm to throw a bottle but thankfully there were still one or two in the gallery who had kept their heads and they stopped him before any damage could be done.

On the 8th green, Still putted up too strongly and watched his ball roll up past the hole and beyond that of his partner's. He then decided to putt it out in order to show Hill the line required, but the canny young Scot Bernard Gallacher, who knows more than a little about golf tactics, decided gracefully to concede Still the putt. At this the excitable Still retaliated by claiming that Britain had forfeited because Gallacher had touched the opposition's ball. The crowd were now almost beyond control. They gave vent to considerable booing, coupled with shouts of 'Go home!' The scene was finally restored to some semblance of order when Dave Hill knocked in his four-foot putt to win the hole and treat the crowd to a mocking bow.

By now British and American officials were rushing to the heated scene in an effort to calm down their men and silence the crowd. During the 9th, 10th, 11th and 12th holes the crowd, although now a little more controlled, still found occasion to boo and shout at the Americans. At the 13th Still put his tee shot in a bunker and yells of 'Good' came from the gallery. This did not amuse Still who shouted back, 'In America we treat you like kings, but here you treat us like tramps.'

At the 15th hole Nicklaus, Sikes, Littler and Douglass came out to urge on Still and Hill; a couple of policemen arrived on the

85

scene too, and this had a settling effect on the crowd and players
alike. Despite all the commotion, the golf was of a very high
standard with the Americans holding on to their lead which was
now only one hole. It stayed this way up to the 17th when Dave
Hill hit two enormous shots down the 17th fairway to be on the
green in 2. He made no mistake with the 12-foot putt and the
eagle 3 was good enough to win the match for the American pair.
Hill was the only player not to shake hands with the referee at the
end of the match. His wife tried hard to make him change his
mind, 'Come on, Dave, we don't want any hard feelings.' To which
Hill replied, 'It's a matter of principle, babe!'

The overall score now read Great Britain 7, United States 7.

When Bembridge and Hunt came to the last green after four
hours and fifty-five minutes of a tight, tense struggle with Aaron
and Floyd, the match was all square. This really had been a close
one, the Americans had gone 1 up at the 3rd and it was not until
the 16th that another hole changed hands, and then the home
team levelled the match. Now with darkness falling, they made
their way by the lights of the club house to the 18th green. Here
Bembridge was left with a five-foot putt for the match, yet although
he could see the hole, the light was making it increasingly difficult
to read the correct line for the putt. It was a sympathetic groan
from the crowd when he missed and Great Britain had to settle
for a half. The score now read 7½-7½.

By the time the final match between Jacklin-Coles and Trevino-
Barber reached the 18th green the light had almost gone: they were
playing the hole by memory. First Coles, bidding for a birdie,
failed; then Jacklin, who had pitched remarkably close consider-
ing the fast-gathering gloom, missed his four-footer. America's
Lee Trevino, who had splashed out of a bunker to be fractionally
under four feet, also missed. Finally Miller Barber, still, strangely
enough wearing his dark glasses, had a 40-inch putt to win the
match—he missed as well.

This was an incredible finish to a match when one considers
three putts of around four feet were missed by three world class
golfers—vital putts which could have swung the match either way.
Quite obviously the light and not their golfing touch had failed
these players in their hour of need.

Britain and America, after an unbelievable day of tension and

Ken Still urges in a birdie putt with his fist clenched and his face screwed up—an attitude which he adopted on more than one occasion during the afternoon battle with Huggett and Gallacher. And sometimes it was not the ball which received this treatment.

drama were locked together at 8 points each. The stage was set for a sensational last day.

After-match comments

When the last putt was sunk, Eric Brown said, 'I'm more than satisfied with the score as it stands because it is so rare that we've gone into the last day without being behind. Huggett was magnificent all day and played his heart out, as did Jacklin, Townsend and Coles. . . . I could go on forever but I will just say I know my boys will give of their best to-morrow in the singles.'

For the American team Sam Snead followed with, 'It's been a hell of a match and I'm looking forward to the singles. Your boys played really well, Huggett and Townsend especially. I don't want to take anything away from the British, but I think my boys failed to make several important putts.'

'Bad man' Still, who had incurred the crowd's wrath, almost broke down when he said, 'I thank God I have this gift to play golf. I've come from nothing, eaten from paper-covered tables. This is our livelihood, it's tough, we are all tough pros. I got shook up and I'm real sorry.'

Hill, his partner, decided it was not the time to make a comment on that explosive match. Huggett said, 'Despite the booing I'd like to say what a great golfer Dave Hill is—no one can take that away from him.'

Bernard Gallacher, the other member of the quartet, said quietly, 'I gave that putt to Still so that he couldn't show the line to his partner, who was putting for a birdie. It is normal golf tactics. We were the best of friends afterwards, it all happened in the heat of the moment. Many things were said which are best forgotten. I know we lost the next two holes after this flare-up but it didn't have anything to do with this: they just happened to get the ball into the hole in fewer strokes. I was not surprised by the outburst. Let's not kid ourselves, America produces tough, determined golfers: it's the hardest school in the world. The competition is terrific, it takes plenty of guts to play well over there.'

Dai Rees, Henry Cotton and Lord Derby in buggie. In the right foreground is pretty Patti Beard, wife of Frank Beard. Here she is following her husband's fourball foursomes match against Butler and Townsend.

Sad note

The very popular caddie Willie Aitchison, who was carrying Trevino's bag in the last match, slipped in the dark when leaving the 17th green and broke his ankle. 'I leaned forward to stop a small child from falling,' explained Willie, 'I had just steadied her when somebody knocked my bag from behind. The sudden weight shift of the heavy bag tilted me over. I heard a crack and I knew the worst.'

HOLE	1	2	3	4	5	6	7	8	9	Out	10	11	12	13	14	15	16	17	18	In	Total
YARDS	493	427	416	212	358	533	158	459	410	3466	393	412	190	517	202	536	401	510	513	3674	7140
PAR	5	4	4	3	4	5	3	4	4	36	4	4	3	5	3	5	4	5	5	38	74

SECOND DAY—FOURSOMES *Afternoon*

Players

	1	2	3	4	5	6	7	8	9	Out	10	11	12	13	14	15	16	17	18	In	Total
Townsend-Butler	5	4	4	2	3	5	2	4	4	33	4	4	3	5	3	4	3	5	5	36	5 under par
Casper-Beard	4	4	3	3	4	3	3	4	3	32	5	4	2	4	3	4	3	5	4	34	8 under par

U.S. won 2 holes

	1	2	3	4	5	6	7	8	9	Out	10	11	12	13	14	15	16	17	18	In	Total
Huggett-Gallacher	5	4	4	3	3	4	—	4	5	—	4	3	3	4	3	4	4	4			4 under par
Hill-Still	4	4	3	3	3	4	—*	3	4	—	4	4	3	5	3	4	4	3			7 under par

U.S. won 2 and 1 (*Hill and Still mistakenly conceded the hole to G.B.).

	1	2	3	4	5	6	7	8	9	Out	10	11	12	13	14	15	16	17	18	In	Total
Bembridge-Hunt	4	4	3	3	4	5	3	4	4	35	4	4	3	4	3	4	3	5	5	35	4 under par
Aaron-Floyd	4	4	3	3	4	5	3	4	4	34	4	4	3	4	3	4	4	5	5	36	4 under par

G.B. and U.S. halved

	1	2	3	4	5	6	7	8	9	Out	10	11	12	13	14	15	16	17	18	In	Total
Jacklin-Coles	4	3	3	3	4	4	3	4	4	33	4	4	3	4	3	4	4	4	5	35	6 under par
Trevino-Barber	5	4	3	3	3	4	2	4	4	33	4	5	3	4	2	4	4	4	5	35	6 under par

G.B. and U.S. halved

GREAT BRITAIN 0, UNITED STATES 2 (two halved)

DAY TWO—OVERALL TOTAL: GREAT BRITAIN 2, UNITED STATES 3 (three halved)

MATCH TOTAL AFTER TWO DAYS: GREAT BRITAIN 6, UNITED STATES 6 (four halved)

6 THIRD DAY SINGLES

On the morning of the last day, Captain Eric Brown picked his strongest available side for the singles matches. He did this knowing that some of his players were beginning to feel the strain, having admitted they were physically and mentally tired. Battle weary they were indeed, but Brown knew their fighting hearts still had much to offer. After much thought, Brown lined his team up so that the last five players (Butler, O'Connor, Huggett, Coles and Jacklin) were all tried and experienced competitors.

First to go off on the morning of the final day was Peter Alliss and what a start he made as he birdied the first two holes to go 2 up on Lee Trevino. Trevino, unshaken, hit back to square the match at the turn and both were out in 34, 2 under par. Having levelled the match, Trevino set about winning it. He took the lead at the next hole, the 10th, and then matching Alliss stroke for stroke grimly held on until the 16th where he went 2 up, a par 4 being good enough to win the hole. Alliss 2 down with 2 to play, bravely birdied the long 17th but to no avail as Trevino repeated the feat and won the match 2 and 1.

Townsend, who started the day with a fine record, was soon in trouble, though not through any fault of his own. He was 1 under par after 11 holes, good enough golf by most standards, but not when your opponent is Dave Hill. Hill's inspired play was the reason why Townsend found himself 3 down at this stage. The one-sided match ended on the 13th where they both dropped birdie putts, Hill's winning margin being 5 and 4.

Also on the course, Neil Coles was having a tremendous battle with Tommy Aaron; one down at the 16th he holed a 15-foot putt for a birdie 3 to take the hole and level the match. Coles, usually unemotional, showed his delight with a victory uppercut. But there were even better things in store for Coles for at the very next hole, the long 17th, he hit the shot of the year and probably his lifetime, when he hammered a 4-wood to within inches of the hole. It was too much for Aaron, and Coles went into the lead. The 18th was halved and Great Britain had picked up their first point of the morning.

Meanwhile Brian Barnes looked set to give Great Britain another

Brian Barnes urges on an eagle putt at the 18th green in his match
against Casper. The ball stopped short inches from the hole.
Casper sunk his putt to win the match by one hole.

victory. He was 2 up playing the 15th, when Casper hit him with a
birdie streak, although some have said it was a lucky streak.
Casper, fighting to stay in the match, pulled his drive at the
15th, it landed in one of the left-hand bunkers and popped out
again. This meant Casper was able to take a wood for his second
shot on this long par 5. He left it 100 yards from the green. He
followed this with a magnificent pitch shot which stopped inches
from the flag. Barnes who was also on in 3, left his putt short and
so conceded the hole.

From the tee at the 16th, Barnes landed in the rough on the
left-hand side. He could only knock it out towards the green: as
for Casper, he was on in 2 to sink another long birdie putt to
square the match. On the 17th, Barnes, looking for a birdie,
let fly a really big one off the tee. This time he caught the rough

P.G.A. chairman Geoffrey Cotton (*far left*) and Lord Derby, president of the P.G.A., sit next to the unluckiest man at Birkdale, caddie Willie Aitchison, who broke his leg the day before and struggled to the course on crutches to watch the final stages of the drama.

on the right-hand side. Casper, who was in the middle of the fairway, had no trouble in reaching the green and sinking another birdie putt to go 1 up.

At the long 18th Barnes hit one of his best drives of the match: Casper not so fortunate had landed in trouble in the right-hand rough. At the previous two holes Barnes had been severely punished for his wayward tee shots, but when I peered at Casper's ball, it was lying in the one bare patch for yards. 'The luck in golf can be cruel,' said Tom Barnes, Brian's father, who was standing beside me. Casper, who was nicely set up to go for the green, did so and registered his fourth successive birdie. Poor Barnes also birdied the 18th, but it was not good enough, the victory was Casper's by one hole.

But it was not all gloom for the spectators. O'Connor was play-

American Ken Still is seen here querying with the referee the fact that the mark of the old hole is in his line of putt. The referee told him there was nothing he could do about it, so Still was forced to putt out in his singles match with Maurice Bembridge.

Ken Still blasts out of a bunker at the 18th during his needle match with Maurice Bembridge. The sand flies but Still keeps his eyes firmly fixed on the ball.

ing inspired golf against Frank Beard. A magnificent wood from the rough on the first hole gave O'Connor a winning birdie 4. Then un-Christy-like he three-putted to lose the 2nd missing from less than three feet. But nothing upsets O'Connor; he bounced back at the short 4th where his tee shot nearly split the pin, to take the hole. He also took the 5th with a shot that ruled the flag all the way, landing 24 inches from the hole.

O'Connor lost the next hole, the 6th, but he righted matters when he slotted in a 10-foot putt on the 7th. Then, when he took

By throwing his hat in the air, the 'baddie' of the series, Ken Still,
sardonically acknowledges the cheers of the crowd at the 18th
after playing out of a bunker in his singles against Bembridge.
Bembridge won by one hole.

With his hands on his hips, Tony Jacklin watches as Jack
Nicklaus lets one go from the tee.

the 8th with another magnificent second shot to the green, he was
3 up on Beard and heading for a big win. When O'Connor's putter
is hot, there is no golfer in the world who can hold him and Beard
was soon to find this out. The Irishman won the 11th and 13th
with birdies and sunk another 8-foot putt for a half at the 14th.
He had no more to do, he had beaten Frank Beard 5 and 4, the
most convincing win so far in the series.

Maurice Bembridge was playing his part magnificently. He
was 4 up with 6 to play, but lost four of the next five holes to
struggle to the 18th all square. The prospect of losing on the final
green did not haunt Bembridge for long, for as it turned out Still
was the one to crack. He found a greenside bunker, much to the
delight of the crowd who still hadn't forgotten his antics of the
previous day, splashed out and finished up taking a 6. Bembridge

Are British galleries unsporting? This picture gives the answer and it's a positive 'NO'. It is plain to see here that they have shown their appreciation of a good putt sunk from the edge of the green by American Jack Nicklaus in his morning match against Tony Jacklin.

had won. With a huge grin he acknowledged the crowd's roar and walked in to a very late lunch, a happy but very tired young man.

Butler was 2 ahead after thirteen holes against Ray Floyd. This safety margin was halved when Floyd won the 14th, but Peter clung on with halves at the 15th, 16th and 17th. Their battle, like so many had before, went to the 18th green for a decision. Butler, who knew he had only to halve the hole to win, did just that and Great Britain finished the morning having won five of the eight matches played.

The Butler-Floyd cliffhanger was the last match to be finished for Jacklin had already won his match, hammering the 'Golden Bear' Jack Nicklaus 4 and 3. This game, which gathered the

Two up in his match against Jack Nicklaus, Jacklin plays from a tricky lie at the 10th during the morning round. Jacklin went on to beat the blond giant at the 15th green.

biggest crowd of the day, saw Nicklaus miss three putts of two feet. Apart from this it was as everybody expected, a classic.

Jacklin reached the turn in 34 to be 2 up on Nicklaus. The Open champion then smartly won the 12th to go 3 up. Although Nicklaus managed to halt the slide temporarily by winning the 13th, Jacklin regained his three-hole lead at the next hole when Nicklaus missed a two-foot putt. The crowd, who had never been quiet throughout this match, applauding both players with equal fervour, went delirious when Jacklin slotted in the birdie putt on the 15th green which beat the blond giant.

THIRD DAY—SINGLES

HOLE	1	2	3	4	5	6	7	8	9	Out	10	11	12	13	14	15	16	17	18	In	Total
YARDS	493	427	416	212	358	533	158	459	410	3466	393	412	190	517	202	536	401	510	513	3674	7140
PAR	5	4	4	3	4	5	3	4	4	36	4	4	3	5	3	5	4	5	5	38	74

Players

Morning

Player	1	2	3	4	5	6	7	8	9	Out	10	11	12	13	14	15	16	17	18	In	Total
Alliss	4	3	4	3	4	5	3	4	4	34	5	4	3	4	3	5	5	4			2 under par
Trevino	5	4	4	3	4	5	2	4	3	34	3	4	3	4	3	5	4	4			5 under par
U.S. won 2 and 1																					
Townsend	4	4	4	3	4	5	3	4	5	36	4	3	5	5	3						1 over par
Hill	4	4	4	3	3	4	3	3	4	32	4	4	4	4	3						4 under par
U.S. won 5 and 4																					
Coles	5	3	3	3	4	4	3	4	4	34	4	c	4	5	3	5	3	3	4	—	3 under par
Aaron	5	4	3	3	4	4	2	4	4	35	5	4	3	4	3	5	4	4	4	36	3 under par
G.B. won 1 hole																					
Barnes	4	4	4	3	4	4	3	c	4	—	4	4	2	5	3	5	5	5	4	37	1 under par
Casper	4	4	5	4	3	5	3	4	4	36	4	4	3	4	4	4	3	4	4	34	4 under par
U.S. won 1 hole																					
O'Connor	4	5	4	3	3	6	2	4	4	35	4	3	3	4	3						3 under par
Beard	6	4	4	4	5	5	3	5	4	40	4	4	3	5	3						4 over par
G.B. won 5 and 4																					
Bembridge	4	3	4	3	4	5	3	4	4	34	4	4	3	5	4	c	4	5	4	—	1 under par
Still	5	4	4	3	4	5	3	4	4	36	4	5	4	4	3	—	4	4	6	—	1 over par
G.B. won 1 hole																					
Butler	5	4	4	3	4	4	2	4	5	35	4	5	3	4	4	5	4	5	4	38	1 under par
Floyd	5	4	4	3	4	5	3	4	5	37	4	4	3	5	3	5	4	5	4	37	level par
G.B. won 1 hole																					
Jacklin	4	4	4	3	4	5	3	4	3	34	4	4	3	4	3	4					4 under par
Nicklaus	4	4	4	3	4	6	3	4	4	36	4	4	4	3	4	6					1 over par
G.B. won 4 and 3																					

GREAT BRITAIN 5, UNITED STATES 3

In the last match to be finished in the morning round, Peter Butler knew he had only to halve the 18th hole to win. He took no chances and did just that. Great Britain finished the morning having won five of the eight matches played.

AFTERNOON THIRD DAY SINGLES

At lunchtime, Eric Brown, with a beaming grin on his face, said that he was delighted with Britain's performance in the morning play. 'Before play began I would have settled for four-all in the morning.' As it was Britain were 2 ahead. All they needed now was $3\frac{1}{2}$

points out of the 8 played for in the afternoon, to win. This was still a demanding task when one considers that on the previous two days the Americans had done far better in the afternoon rounds.

For the afternoon singles the two Peters, Townsend and Alliss, who had lost their matches in the morning were dropped. Their places were filled by Gallacher and Huggett.

Bembridge, who had narrowly beaten Still in the morning, looked desperately tired in his clash with Miller Barber. The golf in this match never reached a high standard, a fact underlined when one considers that Barber did not beat par once on the first nine holes, yet found himself 4 up. Barber went on to win the next three holes to run out the easiest of winners by 7 and 6.

As one would expect this was the first match to finish. Now the margin between the two teams had narrowed to 1 point and from the British point of view worse was still to come.

Barnes, who had been so unlucky in the morning against Casper, could do little right in his afternoon battle with Dave Hill. The good-looking American was out in 33 against the par of 36, and Barnes, who was always struggling in this match, was 3 down. At no time did it look as if Barnes would make a fight of it and Hill needed only to shoot pars to win the 15th and 16th holes to square the points tally for the entire match with his 4 and 2 win.

With the score level the initiative was definitely with the Americans who were now leading in four of the other six matches being played out on the course.

It was now, thanks to the young competent Scot, Bernard Gallacher, that Britain began to hit back. Competing in his first Ryder Cup match, Gallacher played with the calm assurance of a veteran. He hit successive birdies at the 8th and 9th to turn 1 up on his American opponent Lee Trevino. Gallacher's outward half of 33 was flawless golf: he was striking the ball well and missing nothing on the greens. For the first time in the series, Trevino was not smiling: he knew he had a fight on his hands and by the time the 15th green was reached, Trevino had all but lost. Gallacher had a six-foot putt across the slope of this green to win the match. In such a position, Gallacher is not in the habit of slipping up and he did not this time. He rapped the ball into the middle of the hole for a convincing 4 and 3 victory over Trevino. 'I was so determined to win, I could have beaten anybody,' said

the likable Scot after the match.

Butler, in his match against the tall, slim American Dale Douglass, was off to a blistering start, 3 up after four holes, he looked to be heading for a big win; but Americans don't give up that easily and by the time the 10th hole was reached, Douglass had managed the impossible: he had squared the match. The fight was now on—the next two holes were halved and then Butler really got down to it, he won the next three holes in a row, two of them birdies, and eventually ran out an easy winner 3 and 2.

O'Connor, who had hammered the bespectacled Frank Beard in the morning (he was 3 under par when he won on the 14th), was never able to produce the same form in the afternoon against the quiet, slim American Gene Littler. Christy, troubled by his shoulder, was never ahead in this match, although repeatedly behind. He lost the first two holes to birdies, managed to get one back at the 3rd and then, when Littler missed the target on the 6th, squared the match.

But the American went 1 up again at the 9th, 2 up at the 11th, and 3 up at the 12th. O'Connor looked doomed, but he is never one to give up without a fight, and he came storming back with a birdie at the 13th where he reached the green with a drive and a 6-iron.

Although they were both bunkered at the 14th, O'Connor played the better recovery shot and sank a six-foot putt to reduce the deficit to 1. For one moment it looked as if Christy might pull off the miracle, but only for a moment. They both three-putted the 15th for a half in sixes. On the 16th, O'Connor found sand again and dropped back to 2 behind. He could manage no better than a half at the 17th where he went through the green with his second shot; the fighting Irishman had been beaten 2 and 1.

Coles, who had put up such a brave show in the morning when beating Tommy Aaron, found he could not match the long-hitting Dan Sikes. He was always behind in this match. At no time did he play as we know Coles can, being 40 at the turn and 3 down. The last six holes were something of a formality with the American winning three of them for a convincing 4 and 3 win for the United States.

Now there were only two matches still alive for Britain to find the 1½ points needed for victory. Brian Huggett was 1 down to

A jubilant Eric Brown congratulates Bernard Gallacher on his magnificent 4 and 3 victory over Lee Trevino, Britain's first point in the afternoon round.

Billy Casper with 3 to play. Tony Jacklin and Jack Nicklaus were level and the match itself was all square at 15–15.

Huggett, who had been rested in the morning singles, was having a tough, dour battle with Casper; there had never been more than a hole difference between these two players. At this moment in time Huggett was hanging on for his life. He had gone 1 down at the 10th and the position was unchanged when they came to the 16th. It was here hope sprang anew for Britain— Casper twice found sand and Huggett managed to pull the match back to all square.

Unfortunately, ten minutes later, Jacklin lost a hole on the same

Irishman Christy O'Connor plays from the wrong side of the fence in his singles match against Gene Littler. Christy, who was always fighting a losing battle, was eventually beaten 2 and 1.

green to go 1 down in his match against Nicklaus and the overall match position remained unchanged.

As if the golfers out on the course hadn't problems enough, the weather began to play a part. A blustery wind and a spot or two of rain was making the course a sterner test than at any other time during the contest.

At the 510-yard 17th, Casper chipped dead, while Huggett left his chip four-and-a-half feet short. Huggett was now faced with the prospect of sinking this four-and-a-half foot pressure putt in order to scrape a half in a birdie 4. The huge gallery surrounding the green held their breath. Huggett kept his head and

An elated Billy Casper holes a long putt for a birdie-three at the 3rd hole during his singles match against Brian Huggett.

After Billy Casper had holed for a birdie-three at the 3rd, Welshman Brian Huggett coolly followed suit with a similarly long putt and the crowd went wild with excitement.

bravely, oh, so bravely, rapped the ball into the middle of the hole.

Both Huggett and Casper safely negotiated the 18th green in 2. At this point, Jack Nicklaus, in the following match, had hit an enormous 7-iron down the wind, to within 18 feet of the flag at the par-5 17th. Jacklin's second with a 5-iron, was not one of his best. It was helped onto the green by a lucky bounce at the right-hand entrance to the green, and finished up 18 yards from the flag.

Meanwhile back at the 18th, Huggett was faced with a 30-foot putt to win his match with Casper. The green which had now become damp due to the rain, meant that Huggett had to be bold,

Brian Huggett knocks in a four-foot pressure putt on the 18th green to halve his match against Billy Casper. Huggett believed it signalled a victory for Great Britain in the Ryder Cup.

if he was not to leave the putt short. Huggett was bold, perhaps a little too bold, for his ball hurried four and a half feet past the hole. He was now confronted with a tricky return putt to stay alive.

The tension was almost too much as he lined up the return putt and at that precise moment in time, a deafening roar at the 17th green split the heavens. Huggett believed it signalled a victory for Jacklin and he imagined he had to hole this missable putt to win the Ryder Cup for Britain. Displaying visibly the courage which

Emotionally drained Huggett shakes hands with American Billy
Casper after their great encounter.

we have always associated with him, Huggett gritted his teeth,
jutted out his jaw just that little bit more and then literally willed
the ball in. The crowd exploded and Huggett signalled his joy
with a victorious uppercut. Then he walked a little unsteadily to
the side of the green and collapsed in tears on Britain's Ryder Cup
team captain Eric Brown's shoulder.

But Britain had not won the Cup as Huggett had thought: the
big cheer on the 17th green was the signal that Jacklin's huge
55-foot putt for an eagle 3 had dropped. Nicklaus, who was on the
green well inside Jacklin missed his putt so their match was level.

Now Jacklin and Nicklaus were all square with one hole to

On unsteady feet, Brian Huggett falls into the arms of Eric Brown
and unashamedly weeps after his epic match with Billy Casper in
which Brian mistakenly believed he had sunk the putt which had
won the Ryder Cup for Great Britain.

play for the entire match. On the 18th tee both men hit their
drives well. Nicklaus used a 3-wood and was safe just slightly
left of the green. Jacklin, who took a driver, was longer but a
little further to the left of the green. Nicklaus played his approach
shot first: he aimed for the heart of the green and his ball finished
pin high some five yards or so from the flag. Jacklin's approach

Jacklin looks up into the dark sky, a picture of misery, for his putt
had stopped short of the hole on the 18th green during his
(second) crucial singles match against Jack Nicklaus.

American Jack Nicklaus, clearly shows in this picture the concentration he employs when he knows he has a putt he must hole.

shot flew straight at the stick but skidded on past the hole to the back edge of the green. It was Jacklin to putt first some 20 feet from the flag.

The slight drizzle had now made the green both dark and damp. The huge gallery surrounding it were deathly quiet, the tension hung heavy in the air. To watch Jacklin putt demanded

American Jack Nicklaus sinks his second putt on the 18th green. The moment the ball disappeared from sight, Nicklaus walked across and immediately conceded Tony Jacklin's two-foot putt. Then they shook hands after their great match that climaxed the greatest of Ryder Cup matches.

a special brand of courage, for never in the history of British golf has so much depended on one putt. Thankfully the Open champion showed no signs of nerves. He took his time about lining up the putt, then slowly swung back the blade and hit the ball. From the moment it left the clubface it looked a good one, it was straight, but was it strong enough? The answer was no, for it pulled up two feet short of the hole. Britain's victory bid had failed: Jacklin looked up into the dark skies, his putter resting on his shoulder, a picture of misery. One or two women in the crowd unable to hide their disappointment, cried openly.

Nicklaus, who had seen Jacklin's ball pull up on the damp

The greatest ever Ryder Cup match is over and Jack Nicklaus and Tony Jacklin, who had halved their match, walk off the 18th green arm in arm.

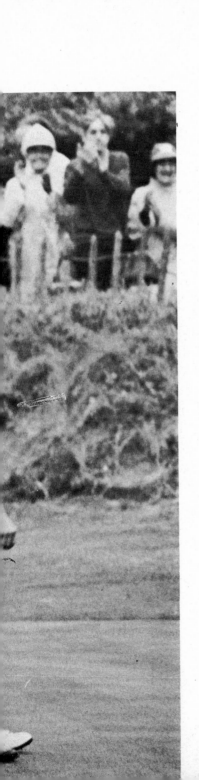

THIRD DAY—SINGLES *Afternoon*

Players	1 493 5	2 427 4	3 416 4	4 212 3	5 358 4	6 533 5	7 158 3	8 459 4	9 410 4	Out 3466 36	10 393 4	11 412 4	12 190 3	13 517 5	14 202 3	15 536 5	16 401 4	17 510 5	18 513 5	In 3674 38	Total 7140 74
Barnes	4	C	4	2	4	6	3	4	5	—	4	5	4	4	4	6	5				6 over par
Hill	4	—	4	3	3	5	3	4	4	—	5	5	3	5	4	5	4				1 over par
U.S. won 4 and 2																					
Gallacher	4	4	3	3	4	5	4	3	3	33	4	5	2	4	3	5					4 under par
Trevino	3	4	4	3	3	5	4	5	4	35	6	4	3	4	4	6					2 over par
G.B. won 4 and 3																					
Bembridge	5	5	4	3	5	6	4	4	6	42	4	5	3								7 over par
Barber	5	4	4	3	4	5	4	4	4	37	3	4	2								1 under par
U.S. won 7 and 6																					
Butler	—	4	4	3	4	6	3	4	4	—	6	4	3	4	3	4	5				1 over par
Douglass	C	5	4	4	3	4	3	4	4	—	5	4	3	5	4	5	5				3 over par
G.B. won 3 and 2																					
O'Connor	5	4	4	3	4	5	3	4	4	36	5	5	3	4	3	6	C	4			2 over par
Littler	4	3	5	3	4	6	3	4	3	35	5	4	2	5	4	6	—	4			level par
U.S. won 2 and 1																					
Huggett	4	4	3	3	3	5	3	3	5	34	5	4	3	4	4	5	—	4	4	—	3 under par
Casper	3	4	3	4	5	5	3	3	4	34	4	4	3	4	4	5	C	4	4	—	3 under par
G.B. and U.S. halved																					
Coles	5	6	4	3	4	6	3	4	5	40	4	4	4	5	3	5					5 over par
Sikes	5	5	4	3	4	5	4	4	4	38	3	6	3	4	3	5					2 over par
U.S. won 4 and 3																					
Jacklin	5	5	4	3	4	4	3	3	6	37	5	4	3	4	3	5	5	3	4	36	1 under par
Nicklaus	5	5	4	2	4	6	3	4	5	38	4	4	4	4	3	5	4	4	4	36	level par
G.B. and U.S. halved																					

GREAT BRITAIN 7, UNITED STATES 7 (two halved)

OVERALL RESULT: GREAT BRITAIN 13, UNITED STATES 13 (six halved)

GREAT BRITAIN 16 points
UNITED STATES 16 points

MATCH RESULT TIE

green, decided to charge the hole, he was looking for a win and he meant to get it. Jack struck the ball well but it never really looked like going in and it raced past some four feet. In the morning matches Nicklaus had missed three putts of around two feet, so one could imagine the thoughts that went through his head when he lined up the return putt, knowing he had this to lose the entire match. But Nicklaus is a truly great champion and when the chips are down he can be relied upon to pull out that something extra. Thankfully for America he did it now. Having satisfied himself with the line, he crouched over the putt and with absolutely no fuss the ball was stroked confidently towards the hole. The moment the ball disappeared from sight, Nicklaus walked across and immediately conceded Jacklin's two-foot putt.

As Nicklaus and Jacklin embraced on the green, a sad face looked on. It belonged to British captain Eric Brown. In the excitement of the closing matches he had lost count of the points situation and his hasty arithmetic had told him that Britain had been pipped at the post by half a point. The moment he realised his error there was no wider grin to be seen in the whole of Lancashire.

Said Tony Jacklin of the last green drama, 'Jack and I are personal friends and I was pleased, really pleased, when he made his last putt. He had his whole country on his back and he holed out like the man he is, then he walked over to me and said, "I would never make you putt that one".'

Before the U.S. team left America, their captain Sam Snead had warned them, 'You won't run over these Limeys because they are good.' After the match Sam Snead joked, 'And they were a damn sight better than I thought they were. This is the greatest golf match you have ever seen in England. This morning I didn't think we were going to take the Cup back.'

Craggy Scot, Eric Brown added, 'I am really proud of my boys— every one of them—I have been saying for months that this team of youth and maturity would give the Americans a hell of a run. I believe that with one or two more youngsters in, we have a wonderful chance of winning before the series is much older.'

7 **LOOKING BACK** QUOTABLE QUOTES FACTS AND FIGURES

Eric Brown and Tom Haliburton were among those dancing a reel in the corridors of the Prince of Wales hotel at 1 a.m. Sunday morning. After stopping for a quick breather, Eric said, 'I made some good and some bad decisions, but most were good.' I'm sure nobody will argue with that.

■ The first two days ended all even with only one match being won by the Americans before the 18th green. This clearly underlined the uphill fight which confronted the Americans in their struggle to keep on even terms.

■ 'I admired the putt Jack Nicklaus hit on the last green,' admitted Alliss, 'he had this one for the entire match and he had a go. It was cold-blooded guts.'

■ TV producer Don Sayer said, 'The script writer did a perfect job.' Those who witnessed the final stages on television will second that.

■ Tony Jacklin played more holes than anyone else over the three days that the Ryder Cup was held . . . 104 out of a possible 108. Neil Coles and Lee Trevino came next, each having played 103 holes.

■ It was estimated that the American Captain Sam Snead and British Captain Eric Brown totalled between them almost 150 miles driving around the course in their electric buggies as they checked the progress of each match in turn.

■ Only two of the American team, Nicklaus and Floyd, were under 30, whereas almost half of the British team, which included the baby of International golf—20-year-old Bernard Gallacher—were 25 or under.

■ Jacklin emerged as the overall star of the contest. He had a total of 35 birdies or eagles and was over par only seven times. He averaged more than one birdie or eagle for every three holes played.

■ In terms of prize money, every one of the United States team had won more in the year 1969 than any one of our players had managed in his golfing lifetime.

■ When asked if he thought the tide had turned and British golf was now catching up with America, Billy Casper replied, 'Definitely, it has now become an even contest.'

■ The night before the final round, Brian Barnes and his attractive wife Hilary, went to see the film *The Battle of Britain*. Said Hilary, 'It was nowhere near as exciting as the battle that went on here today.'

■ After the match, American Miller Barber said, 'This tie is one of the greatest things that has happened to golf in many years: it's a real shot in the arm for the game. You have developed new blood and a new outlook. I would feel we had won if I were British.'

■ When Brian Huggett sank the four-foot putt that halved his vital match with Billy Casper, Eric Brown stayed long enough to embrace him and then dashed off down the fairway. 'After that great cheer that went up for Britain, I thought Jacklin might think that Brian had won his match, so I said to him "We still need you, kid, to win".'

■ 18 of the 32 games were decided on the 18th green, five more did not reach a decision until the 17th and six were decided at the 16th.

■ Ex-Ryder Cup player John Jacobs considered Gene Littler to have the best swing in the American team which, as Jacobs explains, is not surprising since he has been virtually 15 years at the top.

■ 80 per cent of the British balls failed the pre-match test, being too big. Most were 1.70 and it was necessary to go through dozens of boxes before sufficient 1.68 balls were discovered.

SCORES RELATING TO PAR

British Isles	No. of holes played	Under Par	Over Par
Jacklin	104	35	7
Coles	103	26	11
Huggett	87	24	10
Townsend	85	25	7
Bembridge	83	16	11
Butler	70	15	9
Gallacher	67	21	7
O'Connor	67	19	10
Alliss	53	15	4
Barnes	52	13	10
Hunt	36	7	3
Caygill	18	5	0

SCORES RELATING TO PAR

U.S.A.	No. of holes played	Under Par	Over Par
Trevino	103	31	11
Hill	100	24	8
Casper	90	25	11
Aaron	71	16	6
Floyd	70	11	4
Nicklaus	69	17	11
Beard	68	13	8
Barber	64	15	5
Littler	53	17	7
Still	52	13	6
Sikes	51	13	6
Douglass	34	7	6

	Under Par		Par		Over Par		Not played
	G.B.	U.S.A.	G.B.	U.S.A.	G.B.	U.S.A.	
1	20	18	12	12	0	2	
2	4	3	21	24	7	5	
3	8	4	22	25	2	3	
4	3	2	24	25	5	5	
5	5	9	25	21	2	2	
6	10	11	17	17	5	4	
7	5	6	24	23	3	3	
8	6	5	23	24	3	3	
9	4	6	20	22	8	4	
10	5	4	22	22	5	6	
11	3	1	22	26	7	5	
12	2	4	25	24	5	4	
13	21	17	10	10	0	4	1
14	1	1	24	22	6	8	1
15	11	10	14	14	4	5	3
16	6	5	14	18	6	3	6
17	14	11	8	11	1	1	9
18	11	14	7	3	0	1	14

INDIVIDUAL TEAM PERFORMANCES

British Isles	Played	Won	Halved	Lost	Points
Jacklin	6	4	2	0	5
Coles	6	3	1	2	$3\frac{1}{2}$
Townsend	5	3	0	2	3
O'Connor	4	2	1	1	$2\frac{1}{2}$
Bembridge	5	2	1	2	$2\frac{1}{2}$
Gallacher	4	2	0	2	2
Butler	4	2	0	2	2
Huggett	5	1	2	2	2
Caygill	1	0	1	0	$\frac{1}{2}$
Hunt	2	0	1	1	$\frac{1}{2}$
Alliss	3	0	1	2	$\frac{1}{2}$
Barnes	3	0	0	3	0

United States	Played	Won	Halved	Lost	Points
Hill	6	4	0	2	4
Trevino	6	3	1	2	$3\frac{1}{2}$
Littler	3	3	0	0	3
Casper	5	2	2	1	3
Sikes	3	2	0	1	2
Barber	4	1	2	1	2
Aaron	4	1	1	2	$1\frac{1}{2}$
Beard	4	1	1	2	$1\frac{1}{2}$
Nicklaus	4	1	1	2	$1\frac{1}{2}$
Still	3	1	0	2	1
Floyd	4	0	2	2	1
Douglass	2	0	0	2	0

N.B.—Points are allocated to each member of the foursomes and four-ball pairings, so the total points come to more than the 32 at stake.

8 SUMMARY LOOKING FORWARD

'I think they had the stronger reserves,' admitted Eric Brown after the match in front of Sam Snead, 'our boys just didn't stay the distance so well but we can win next time. A few more good youngsters and we will have a hell of a team.'

This statement argues well for our chances in the States, when America defends the Cup in two years time. Their sponsors are already bidding big money (in the region of $100,000 or more) to stage the next event which all America wants to see.

Frank Beard of the U.S. team was quoted as saying he would like to buy the film rights of the match and would be happy to pay $100,000 for it. Not for his own personal film library, he quickly added, but to show it on a world-wide basis. He was confident he could make a profit around the $100,000 mark.

There can be no question that this historic tie was the greatest Ryder Cup match ever staged in the forty-two years the series has been played. In fact, it is doubtful if, in the whole history of sport, there can have been a closer or more drama-packed finish to a contest. Twelve of the sixteen matches on the first two days ended on the last green. Each side won seven singles and the contest, which ran over three days, involving 24 players in 32 separate matches, was not decided until Nicklaus conceded Jacklin's two-foot putt on the 18th green in the last match. The final tally of points was thirteen each to Britain and America with six matches halved—a truly remarkable set of figures.

This result is sufficient proof that the American P.G.A. should reconsider its exemption ruling which permits British Ryder Cup players to compete in only a maximum of six U.S. Tournaments in any one year. It is foolish and wrong to deny these twelve British players the recognition that their fighting hearts have so richly earned them. They should at once be granted full exemption for all U.S.P.G.A. events.

The battle of Birkdale has proved the turning point in British golf: we can look to the future with confidence. Sam Snead generously admitted that he felt the British team had, if anything, played better than the Americans. Britain, it was generally agreed, deserved more than a tie, so we in this country can comfort ourselves with the thought that we gained, at least, a moral victory.

The American P.G.A.'s gesture to allow Britain to hold the

It's the British team's turn to take a bow and it's laughter all round when Tiny Brian Huggett clambers up on a chair. Appreciative gallery includes the Duke of Norfolk and Earl of Derby (*bottom far left*).

The battle of Birkdale is over but the crowd remain ready to give
one last cheer at the presentation ceremony.

trophy for a year is an acknowledgement of this. Under the Ryder
Cup rules, the Americans as holders, were fully entitled to retain
the trophy, but Leo Fraser, president of the U.S.P.G.A. said
that all the American players were happy to concede a half share
of the Cup.

The trophy will now rest for the next twelve months at the
P.G.A. offices at the Oval—for the first time since Britain's out-
right victory in 1957. Let's hope that after 1971 its stay will be a
longer one.